Discover Grassington and Upper Wharfedale

A Practical Guide for Visitors by

Edward Gower

Dalesman Books
1985

THE DALESMAN PUBLISHING COMPANY LTD.
CLAPHAM, via Lancaster, LA2 8EB

First published in this format, 1985
© Edward Gower, 1977, 1985

ISBN: 0 85206 832 8

MAIN STREET, GRASSINGTON

Printed by Fretwell & Brian Ltd.
Goulbourne Street, Keighley, West Yorkshire BD21 1PZ

Contents

Drawings by Edward Gower. Maps by Edward Gower (page 4) and
J. J. Thomlinson (page 16).

Photographs by F. Leonard Jackson (p. 29); W. R. Mitchell (p. 2);
Robert Rixon (p. 20); Clifford Robinson (p. 9, 24).

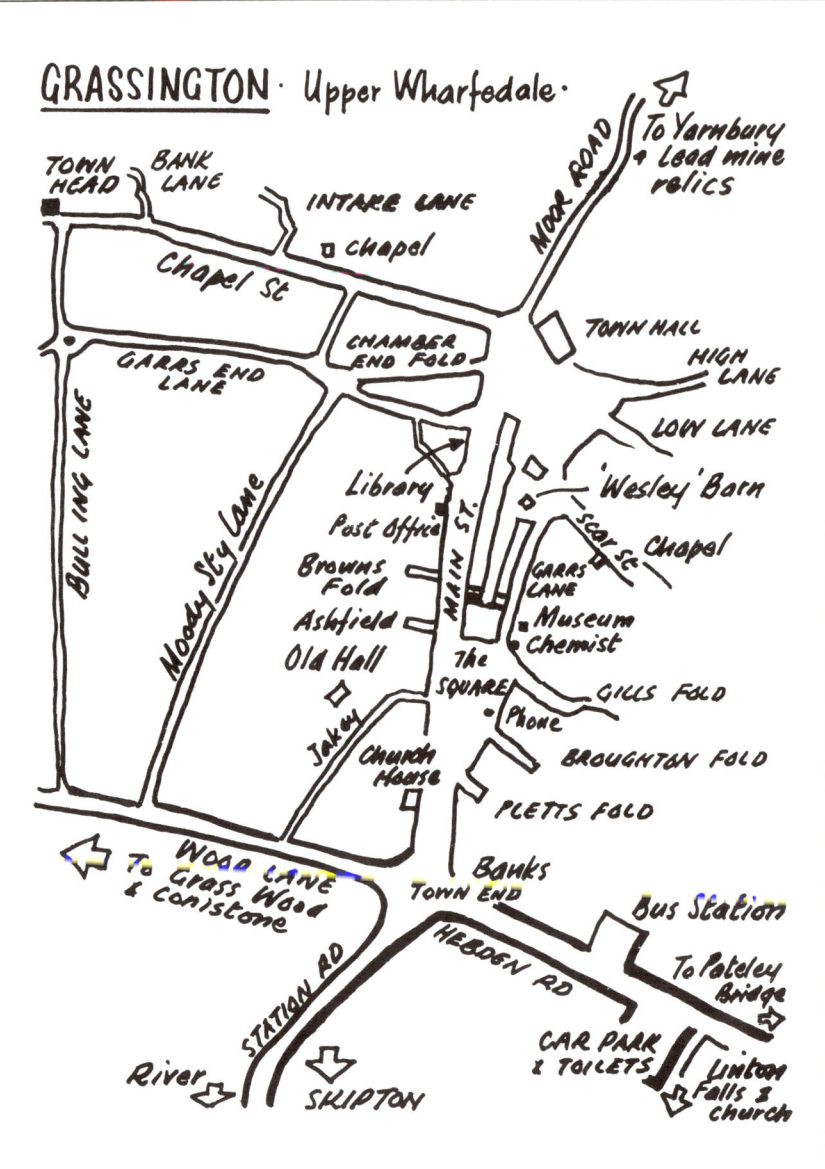

Grassington

In the Square

IF you visit Grassington on a fine Sunday in summer, or on a Bank Holiday, the Square will be a seething mass of people with cars parked on every square foot of cobbles. There will probably be a queue at the bakers, and another one for ice cream. The bars in the hotels will be so busy that raising one's elbow can be difficult. The seats will be full of resting elderly visitors; walkers crowd around the shops; strangers ask directions from anyone who looks like a local. Yet in the throng a tractor makes slow way with a trailer loaded with hay bales behind it. A reminder that this is still a Dales village, and that only five minutes' walk away is beautiful, unspoilt, quiet countryside.

Grassington is the "capital" of Upper Wharfedale. It seems to have been so for centuries. Probably the convergence of roads from other parts of the Dales has something to do with it. The lead mining industry which flourished here made it a centre. The railway helped in the early 1900s, and the village's close proximity to the industrial centres of the county makes it an easy drive for modern motorists, who find the quaint old houses round the cobbled square very attractive.

General Information

Grassington was from medieval times in the West Riding of Yorkshire. When the Ridings were abolished in 1974 with local government re-organisation, the village became part of the new county of North Yorkshire, which is the largest in England. Grassington is in the Yorkshire Dales National Park, which has an area of 680 square miles. The full postal address is Grassington, Skipton, North Yorkshire.

Craven is the ecclesiastical name for a large area centred on Skipton, the full name of the town being Skipton-in-Craven. Some villages also have the appendage, such as Linton-in-Craven, of which parish Grassington is part.

Population: About 1,200.

Early closing: Thursday.

Post Office: Main Street. Phone Kiosks in the Square and in the Car Park.

Garages and petrol at Town End.

Inns: The Black Horse, The Devonshire and the Foresters Arms.

Churches: Parish Church at Linton; Methodist and Congregational in the village; Roman Catholic church at Threshfield.

Banks: Town End.

Police: Opposite Wilson Arms Hotel, Threshfield.

Youth Hostel at Linton.

Museum: In the Square. Open — April to September, 2 p.m. to 4.30 p.m. Winter — Tuesday, Thursday, Saturday, Sunday, 2 p.m. to 4.30 p.m. Evening lectures for visitors.

Buses: Regular service to Skipton from bus station on Hebden Road. Less frequent service to Kettlewell and Buckden in summer; also to Nidderdale, Ilkley and to Wensleydale on summer weekends.

Nearest rail station: Skipton.

Toilets and main car park: Hebden Road, opposite bus station.

Recreation Angling — Trout and grayling on river Wharfe. Day tickets from Post Office. Golf, tennis, swimming, etc., in Skipton (9 miles). Guided walks from National Park Centre.

Library: Top of Main Street.

Upper Wharfedale Fell Rescue H.Q.: Hebden Road.

Caravans and camping: No sites in the village. Nearest at Long Ashes (Threshfield), Wood Nook, Skirethorns (Threshfield), Threaplands (Cracoe), Arncliffe or Appletreewick.

The Yorkshire Dales National Park authority seeks to preserve the natural beauty of the area and to help visitors enjoy it. At the same time it endeavours to protect the farmer and landowner from vandals and trespassers. Much of the park is privately owned, and access is by road, bridle road or footpath, except on the open fell. Most farmers are friendly, so long as the visitor respects their livelihood.

A National Park Centre is adjacent to the National Park Office. Entrance is directly from the car park on Hebden Road. First time visitors will find much valuable information in the Centre.

A Brief History

There was a settlement at Grassington in the Bronze Age, and there are extensive remains of an Iron Age village a short distance to the north. The tribe known as the Brigantes, who resisted the Roman invasion, were active in the area. Fort Gregory, used by the Brigantes, is at the top of Grass Wood. There is evidence of a Roman road across the top of the village, which possibly ran from Ilkley (Olicana) to Wensleydale. The Anglian village was built around the stream, which now flows under the Square. At the time of the Norman Conquest the name was Ghersintone, and the local name is still close to it — Girston.

The ownership of the manor passed from the Plumptons to the Cliffords, then to the Cavendish family, and the Dukes of Devonshire.

A market charter was granted in 1281, and a Michaelmas Feast is still observed, although the date has been altered by a few days. The lead mining industry enlarged the village in the 18th and 19th centuries.

Always a centre for Upper Wharfedale, Grassington is now one of the most popular places in the Yorkshire Dales National Park. It has a selection of shops, inns, guest houses and several cottages offering bed and breakfast. Although there are furnished holiday cottages and flats to let, it is not a commuter village and still has a lively social life. There are several farms on the fringes, with sheep on the higher land and dairy cattle lower down. Grassington is a good centre for walking, touring and a favourite area for potholers.

Distances: Skipton 9 miles; Ilkley 15 miles; Keighley 18 miles; Bradford 28 miles; Leeds 32 miles.

Books: Life and Tradition in the Yorkshire Dales, Hartley and Ingilby (Dent).
    A History of Grassington, Susan D. Brooks (Dalesman).
    Wharfedale (Dalesman).
    The Yorkshire Dales (Dalesman).
    Exploring the Yorkshire Dales, E. Gower (Dalesman).
    Walking in the Craven Dales, C. Speakman (Dalesman).
Map: O.S. Sheet 98.

TOM LEE's "SMIDDY".

In the Old Village

From the bridge over the river Wharfe, the road climbs steeply up Station Road to Town End, where roads lead off to Kettlewell and Pateley Bridge. At the corner a white painted building housing Barclays Bank was once an inn called The Jobbers Arms. A little way up the Main Street is a smithy, once the scene of clanging hammer and glowing forge, and now in use again.

Town End was once much narrower than now. Where the garden of the baker's shop hides behind its stone wall was a great barn. The building now the Gallery was a barn before being converted by a local potter who could be seen at his wheel through the large window.

On the left, going up, the baker's shop is part of a large 19th century house, and next to it the grocers was once a barn and stables for the horse buses and charabancs. Known as the Royal Mail Livery Stables, it was owned by Kit Chapman who had forty horses. His mail coach left Grassington at 5.45 a.m. for Skipton. No wonder the blacksmith was handy. Next to the grocers is Church House, used by the clergy for some functions to save the journey to the parish church which is across the river at Linton. This fine old building has a carved stone over the door — S.A.P. 1694. It was built as a farm house for Stephen and Alice Peart, who were fairly prosperous local farmers. The ground floor has mullioned windows, and inside, although altered somewhat, the large rooms still given an idea of life in the 17th century.

Opposite Church House the shops have been made from old cottages. Quite recently the Nook lost a projecting upper window, while the wool shop next door once had a stone outside staircase.

Pletts Fold, which leads off to the right by the sheepskin shop, is one of several such "folds" in the village. They are sometimes called "yards" in other Yorkshire towns, and were developed, as gardens or crofts were filled in by new houses. Often the houses were built for sons or daughters on marriage. The nearness helped family unity, and the buildings kept out the cold winter winds. There is a Georgian house at the end of the fold, and a dated doorhead — H.E.A. 1744.

The group of old cottages next to the sheepskin shop has some quaint windows. Then comes Broughton Fold, with Grassington House to the left. This fine Georgian building was built by Mr. Brown, who was one of the promoters of the Grassington to Pateley turnpike road. The Allcock family, bankers in Skipton, lived there for many years. Their large garden behind the house is now the car park for the hotel. When it became a "boarding establishment," the proprietor advertised: "Donkeys for hire. Liveried coachman to meet trains at Skipton or Bolton Abbey."

Next to the gent's outfitters, which has been altered a great deal, is Jacob's Fold. From here a narrow way under trees leads by the wall of the Old Hall into Wood Lane. This is still called "Jakey" by local people, and gives glimpses of the older parts at the back of the Devonshire Hotel. Behind the

Grassington roofscape, showing the jumble of cottages and houses. This view from the top end of the village looks across Wharfedale towards Skirethorns.

wall is Grassington's oldest house. The Old Hall is said to be 14th century, although some authorities doubt this. It was the home of the Plumpton family; Peter de Plumpton was a Norman baron. The extensive gardens are white with snowdrops in spring and the tall trees, which overhang "Jakey," are busy with rooks whose cacklings can often be heard in the Square.

At the top of the Square, which is really a triangle, is a large 19th century building, shown on old photographs as a warehouse and originally a tannery. After the railways brought the visitors, it was a popular cafe. Liverpool House, as it was known, advertised: "Genuine drugs and fancy snuffs; Provision dealer and general draper. Every article in the general drapery trade kept in stock." To the right of this, the chemist has a charming bow window frontage, but this is a modern alteration and the plain fronted original house was once the local telephone exchange. The house on the corner of Hardy Grange was the manor house.

The Square was recobbled in 1973, the money being raised by the local Chamber of Trade which organises an annual exhibition of Yorkshire Dales Arts and Crafts in August. There were more trees in the Square at one time, one of them dying, so it is said, from fumes given off by the traction engines of the travelling fair which occupied the Square in October for the annual

"Feast." The old pump, which has been moved from its original position, has two troughs and was in use in living memory. The beck from the moor runs in a culvert under the Square and joins the river a short way below the bridge.

Walking up Main Street, we see on the left a white painted shop, now a fruit shop. This was the "smiddy" of Tom Lee, who about 1767 murdered the local doctor in Grass Wood as he was returning from Kilnsey. A little higher, by the Post Office, is Neddy Hill, originally Salt Pie Hill, where the village salt supply was unloaded. Here, many years ago, old Bowes mended clogs and cut a man's hair for 2d. When shaving a customer, he did not use a towel or cloth to wipe off the lather, but flung it from the razor across the room into the fireplace. He also read head "bumps" and foretold the future. The cafe on the left has a quaint tunnel leading into Garrs End Lane, by way of "The Woggins."

Nearly at the top of the street is Chamber End Fold, or King Street, with a 17th century house at the corner. This narrow street contains old lead miners' houses.

The Town Hall and Devonshire Institute at the top of the street was built in 1855 over the beck where cattle were once watered. The cafe just below was made from old cottages with wells outside and was called Well Head. The waters were said to have medicinal properties.

Chapel Street has more folds. One of them, Chapel Fold or Ranters Fold, has the old Primitive Methodist Chapel now used by a furniture craftsman. At the far end of Chapel Street is Ingle Nook, dated 1628, and Town Head Farm, with mullioned windows and an ornamental border made from pebbles. Turning left, we pass a house on the site of the old manorial mill and come to a junction with a tree in the centre. Cove Lane to the right is sometimes called Fairy Flit, because it leads to a cave on the edge of Grass Wood said to be used by fairies. To the left is Garrs End Lane, which goes back to the Main Street, and in front Bull Ings Lane joins Wood Lane.

Back in the Square, to the right at the top, is Garrs Lane, narrow and having old cottages on one side and the Congregational Chapel and graveyard on the other. The chapel was built in 1812. Facing the graveyard, the top cottages were once the Theatre where Tom Airey, the actor, manager and local carrier, had such prominent players as Edmund Kean in his productions. Scar Street, on which the chapel stands, is thought to be on the site of a Roman road. Just round the corner to the left is Pletts Barn, now "The Mountaineer", often called Wesley Barn. This splendid old building, with its arched ventilation slits and pigeon cote, has a date 1683. Wesley is said to have preached either in it or in front of it.

The Museum is in the Square. It was officially opened on July 1st, 1979, by Robert Crowther, of California, U.S.A., grandson of the late John Crowther, a well known antiquarian and botanist, who had a small museum in Grassington in the 1900s. It has a relief map of old Grassington and many items of lead mining, farming and domestic interest.

The Bridge

At the bottom of Station Road is Grassington Bridge, once called Linton Bridge. This splendid structure carries traffic today that its builders never dreamed of. There must have been a ford here in ancient times, and eventually a wooden bridge. The cottage to the left on the Threshfield side, called "Lady Well Cottage," could have been a hostel for travellers to Kilnsey in the times when the abbeys were powerful. Its steep roof indicates it being thatched before the slates were placed.

In 1603 a narrow humpbacked stone bridge was built with a steep climb from it. In the 18th century it was widened and the approaches levelled. Traces of small arches can be seen in the field on the downstream side, as well as the line of the early structure. Under the arches the newer part can be distinguished from the old one. There are mason marks on the stones. It was widened in 1984 to provide a footpath. More information is in the Museum.

Just above the bridge to the right, going down from the village, is a seat under a clump of trees. This is Donkey Hill. It was said that the gibbet used when executing Tom Lee, the blacksmith, was buried here. The manacles and leg irons were placed under one of the bridge buttresses. His body was left hanging by the roadside in Grass Wood, until his bare bones were taken by passing gipsies.

A footpath follows the river downstream to Linton Falls, with two weirs to be passed first. A ruinous structure by the top weir was the generating house of the electricity plant which supplied light to the village. The lower weir, often the haunt of numerous ducks, gathered water for powering the mill, overlooking the falls. The mill was demolished in 1983. The group of cottages is called Botany. Mill workers lived in them when the mill produced textiles.

The narrow bridge, originally "tin bridge," gave access from Grassington to the mill by the paved footpath locally called the "snake walk." It used to be closed on one day a year to establish private ownership.

LADY WELL COTTAGE

Grassington Lead Mines

On the moor above the village are many relics of the industry which was important in the Dales for a long time. If you go up Moor Road, which ascends from the top of Main Street, in about 1½ miles is Yarnbury where the tarmac ends. Protected by wind-battered trees, the cluster of lonely buildings was once the busy centre of the lead mines. There was the office, the agent's (manager's) house, weigh house and a smithy. The large house, derelict for many years, has been renovated. A few yards up the rough moor road, and under it, is a stone arched entrance to an incline with the date 1828.

Walking up this road between high stone walls a wide vista of moorland is soon seen. Across the valley, spoil heaps are scattered and remnants of buildings can be seen. A map board here provides information on the old mines. Prominent to the right is the 40 ft. Cupola smelt mill chimney, which has been restored by a local mining group. Below it are the arched flues which carried the gases to the chimney and radiate in several directions. This mill worked from the 17th century until about 1886.

Turning right at Yarnbury over the cattle grid, a road runs across the moor into Hebden Gill. There are mine shafts to be seen, usually fenced or covered, and very dangerous. No attempt should be made to explore them, and in misty weather or when snow covers the ground they should be avoided. In the Gill there are some ruined buildings and waterways. There was a large waterwheel here for working pumps.

Crossing the dam, the roadway on top of which was eroded in a severe thunderstorm in 1975, the bridleway climbs onto the High Moor to the site of the High Grinding Mill, which was damaged by army gunners in World War II. Work was restarted here in 1955, and new buildings erected for the extraction of fluorspar, but this ceased about 1961.

There was a smelt mill down by the river Wharfe, opposite Linton church, where a beck emerges. This was Low Mill, and traces of it can be seen next to the corn mill, now converted into a dwelling. A lane leads to Low Mill from Hebden Road, about half a mile from Town End.

Lead mining in the Dales was probably carried out before the Roman came. The invaders certainly worked the mines with local labour. "Pigs" have been found in the area date-stamped A.D. 81. Bolton Priory opened lead mines at Stump Cross, on Greenhow Hill, about 1300. There were mines in Grassington in the 17th century, and until the mid-19th century the industry gave work to a large number of people.

Many cottages in the village were occupied by miners, who worked long hours in very unpleasant and dangerous conditions, with poor wages. They had to walk up to the moor and back again. Women and even children were employed on surface jobs. Some of the families had smallholdings with a cow and a few pigs.

The steep part of the Moor Road, below Spring House, is called "Hungry

Laugh Hill," from the returning miners chuckling at the scent of frying bacon from the cottages below. The industry ceased in the 1870s due to the imports of cheaper Spanish lead. Many families left the Dales for the mills of the West Riding or East Lancashire, and some emigrated. It is likely that there are large deposits of lead still under the moor, but whether it would be economically or aesthetically desirable to develop them is a matter for conjecture.

Books: *Lead Mining in the Yorkshire Dales, Arthur Raistrick (Dalesman).*
Mines and t' Miners, J. M. Dickinson.

The Railway

Across the river, at the brow of the hill in Threshfield, is a group of new houses with neo-Georgian windows and doors. They stand on the site of Grassington railway station. The last remains, including the signal box which served the last years of its life as headquarters of the Fell Rescue Association, vanished in 1975. The old lamp adorns the gateway of the new Fell Rescue building in Hebden Road.

The Yorkshire Dales Railway was planned to go to the head of Wharfedale at Kettlewell, and then with a 3½ mile tunnel into Coverdale link with the main York to Darlington line. Economies due to the ending of the railway boom caused the line to end at Grassington. It ran from the junction at Embsay on the Skipton–Ilkley line. After long delays it was opened in July 1902, but never flourished and was closed to passenger traffic by the LMS Railway in 1930. Excursions were run at holiday weekends for many years after this, from Leeds and Bradford, and were very popular. Freight trains continued until 1969 but now the only activities are the special trains to and from the lime works at Swinden. The tracks have been lifted between Swindon and Grassington. There was a station at Rylstone, where the level crossing still operates.

The confectioner's shop on the opposite side of the road is said to have been built in line with the rail head, in the hope that should the railway be continued up the dale the shop would be knocked down and the owner compensated.

The trains revived Grassington, and new houses were built for Bradford wool executives who could travel daily to business. There were connections at Skipton with the Bradford–Morecambe "Residential Express." The row of houses overlooking the bridge was known as "Boiled egg Row," because the wives could see the train approaching the station and begin to prepare the eggs for tea. Grassington began to develop as a holiday resort.

Interesting information about the line can be seen at Embsay Station, where the Yorkshire Dales Railway Preservation Society has some locomotives and other relics, and in Grassington Museum.

Book: *Railways in the Yorkshire Dales, K. Hoole (Dalesman).*

Villages near Grassington

Hebden

(1½ miles from Grassington, on the B6265 Pateley Bridge road)

THIS village, which like Grassington is in the parish of Linton-in-Craven, has some old cottages alongside a beck. This flows from Grassington Moor down Hebden Gill, where there was much lead mining. Some ruined buildings can be seen. The Gill is upstream from the main road bridge; a narrow, surfaced road runs for about a mile to Hole Bottom, and from there a bridleway ascends the moor to Yarnbury. The road then goes down to Grassington.

Hole Bottom, a fine old farmhouse opposite another old building known as Jerry and Ben's, was connected with the lead mines. In the 19th century a family of musicians lived here. Several brothers and their father made up a popular band.

There is a waterfall, Scala Force, reached through a gate about halfway up the Gill. The scenery around is spectacular.

In the lower part of the village, near the little school (now closed), a footpath goes down to the beck, passing the old watercourses which once powered the now demolished mill. The road turning off right from Hebden Bridge leads to the river and on to Burnsall, giving fine views of this village. A footpath crosses a field to a spectacular swing bridge from which paths lead to Burnsall and Thorpe.

Inn: The Clarendon.
Shop and Post Office.
Toilets.

Threshfield

On the other side of Grassington Bridge is Threshfield. The old village is at the top of the rise, with a tall blue silo tower rearing above the trees. It lies between the road from Burnsall and the one that goes up the dale to Kettlewell.

The Park, originally the village green, has some fine trees and is fringed by old cottages. Opposite is the Old Hall hotel, a Georgian building standing in front of the remnants of the original Hall, dating from the 14th century. To the right at the top of the green is a fine house, now called Park Grange, which was built by the Hewitt family in 1640.

14

PARK GRANGE - THRESHFIELD

At the bottom of the row of cottages to the left of the green is the Manor House, which has a Victorian face to the road but round the corner has a fine porch and above it a beautiful rose window of the Tudor period. Over the bridge, which has massive top stones, is Ling Hall. This is a re-building of an old house famous at one time for its besoms. The Ibbotson family made these by the wagon load from heather twigs. Notice the old horse and cow shoes on the barn door.

There is a small chapel at the corner where the Grassington road meets the Kettlewell road. A short way up this latter road is a garage and a filling station. At Long Ashes, a mile or so towards Kettlewell, is a caravan site and Leisure Centre.

The Skipton to Grassington bus passes through Threshfield, on the Burnsall road.

Threshfield Free Grammar School, a fine building dating from 1674, is near the river on the road from Linton Mill to Grassington Bridge. It is reputed to be haunted by Pam the Fiddler, a musical ghost who frightened the schoolmaster.

Inn: The Old Hall Hotel. Petrol station and garage.
Hotel: The Wilson Arms.
Book: Village Schools: An Upper Wharfedale History, Elizabeth Raistrick (Dalesman).

Overleaf: Picture map of Upper Wharfedale, by J. J. Thomlinson. (An enlarged copy of this map, suitable for framing, is published separately by the Dalesman Publishing Company).

Fleet Moss

Beckermonds • **Yockenthwaite** • **Hubberholme** • **Buckden**

Buckden Pike

Hunt

Near the farmhouses of Beckermonds the Wharfe begins where the Oughtershaw Beck joins the Greenfield Beck.

LANGSTROTHDALE

HUBBERHOLME CHURCH

In the old days, the sexton would stand on the tower of Hubberholme church, ready to ring the bell when he caught sight of the parson on his white horse riding over the fells.

Starbotton

Halton Gill

R. Skirfare

Old Cote Moor Top

Litton

Arncliffe

Ket

Littondale

Hawkswick Moor

New Cover Scar

KILNSEY

Situated under the great overhanging crag, Kilnsey grew from a grange owned by the monks of Fountains Abbey, who had extensive sheep grazing pastures in Craven.

Fountains Fell

ARNCLIFFE

Charles Kingsley stayed at Arncliffe and the sparkling river Skirfare together with the infant Aire at Malham, inspired his 'Water Babies'.

Packhorse Bridge
Linton

Malham

Skipton

GRASSINGTON BRIDG

Wharfedale

Wharfe, as he moved along
To matins joined a mournful voice
Nor failed at evensong.

Wm. Wordsworth.

...Stone

...post on the
...te from Coverham
...ttlewell. Legend
...unter's Stone turns round
...clock at Hunter's Hall

...ell

...tel, an Irish Norse
...ttlewell became an
...rket town in the century
...he Norman conquest.

...nsey
...nistone

Many reminders of the once thriving lead mining industry can be found on the fells above Grassington.

BARDEN TOWER Barden Tower originated as a keepers lodge, but it was converted in the 15th Century into a private dwelling place by Henry Clifford ~ the Shepherd Lord.

Bolton Abbey

Grassington
Hebden
...reshfield
Linton
Barden Church
Burnsall
Thorpe

Wharfe

●**Trollers Gill**

Legends abound in this area of the dreaded Barguest, the ghost dog of the Dales, whose appearance foretold disaster. At one time, it was said that every house had a horse shoe over the door as a protection against witchcraft.

Appletreewick

Once renowned for its fair for sheep, horses, and horned cattle, Appletreewick was the birthplace of Sir William Craven. Born to poor parents, he became Lord Mayor of London in the reign of James I

Barden Bridge
The Strid

The narrow chasm of the Strid, where the Wharfe has carved a way through the rocks, is the scene of the legend of the Boy of Egremond. The youth decided to jump the Strid with his greyhound on a leash, the hound held back and the luckless boy fell into the swirling water and was drowned ~

Bolton Bridge

THE GRAMMAR SCHOOL, BURNSALL

Linton

Linton-in-Craven is its full name, and both Grassington and Threshfield are in Linton Parish. Unspoilt by modern buildings, and usually quiet, the village lies round a green with a beck burbling at one side. It has three bridges, the road bridge replacing the ancient clapper bridge which was moved to the top of the village. The middle bridge is a 14th century packhorse structure that was repaired in the 17th century by Dame Elizabeth Redmayne, and it still bears her name.

The inn is called the Fountaine after a famous son of the village. Richard Fountaine left the Dales and made a fortune in London, becoming an alderman of the City. He died in 1721 and provided money for an almshouse in Linton for six poor men and women. The splendid building which dominates the green was the result. Designed by Sir John Vanbrugh, the architect of Castle Howard, it has separate "cottages" for the residents and a chapel. The executors own land in Grassington, Threshfield and Hebden, which provides an income for upkeep of the "hospital" as it is called.

At the bottom of the village across the road is Linton Old Hall, a fine old farmhouse with 17th century windows showing signs of later alterations. Downstream from the bridge is an attractive house with a lawned garden reaching to the beck, where there are stepping stones. This is White Abbey, which was the home of Halliwell Sutcliffe, the writer, whose book *The Striding Dales* has become a minor classic.

The church is by the river Wharfe. The road from Linton goes straight over the crossroads at Bank Top and down the hill, passing the row of cottages where there is a car park. A few minutes' walk along the riverside is the Norman church, with two cottages, "Kirk Yett," at the gate. These were once an inn. The church has some 12th century work and the main fabric is 14th century.

Inn: The Fountaine. Post Office. Youth Hostel.

LINTON CHURCH

18

Short Walks around Grassington

SOME people come and stay in the village, wandering round the Square and walking up the Main Street. This is very pleasant, but to appreciate the beauty of the district it is better to walk a little further. There are hills everywhere, but some are not very steep and the views are always worth the effort. Good footwear is essential. Many of the paths are rough and often muddy.

Linton Falls (½ mile)

Go down the hill from the bottom of the Main Street, turning half right on the main Skipton Road. The river bridge is at the bottom, and on the left side is a stile in the wall. The footpath goes from here on the riverside, where there is space to picnic or places to paddle and swim. There are ledges under the water which can be dangerous, especially to toddlers, and it is wise to watch them. Two weirs are passed, then the falls, with Tin Bridge crossing them. Go through the stile and up the flagged footpath (Snake Walk). This comes out in Hebden Road next to the car park.

Linton Church can be visited by crossing Tin Bridge and going round the corner of the houses, and then turning left. The road leads alongside the far bank of the river to the church, which can be seen from the flagged footpath. By the high wall which surrounds the mill house is Lile Emily's bridge, a small charming stone structure across the beck from Threshfield, usually with many ducks around waiting for bread. Named after Emily Norton, a powerful local family who once owned much land in the district, the bridge is probably much older than Emily and formed part of an ancient way to the church.

It is possible when the river is low to cross the stepping stones below the church, and return by way of Low Mill (opposite the church) up the lane to Hebden Road (1 mile).

The Ghaistrills (1 mile)

Go down to the bridge and, by Donkey Hill on the right, through a gate and into the field. There is an obvious footpath, and in spring, when this field is thick with grass for hay, the path should be adhered to. A little bridge crosses the stream which appears from underground not far away at Braith Gill. Many birds can be seen around here — dippers, wagtails, moorhens, peewits, curlews, blackheaded gulls, and sometimes a heron or a kingfisher.

Very soon the river becomes turbulent, with rocky rapids, and in times of heavy rain is very noisy and spectacular. A little higher the water speeds

Picturesque cottages in the village of Linton. This attractive settlement, unspoilt by modern buildings and usually quiet, clusters round a green with a beck at one side.

through a narrow rocky channel. At one time a man could jump across, but it is impossible now. This is Ghaistrills strid, probably something to do with "ghosts' stride."

Retrace your steps towards the footbridge, but bear left across the field to a stile in the wall, from where a footpath leads to a barn. Go round the back of this, through the gate, and across the field to another gate which opens into Wood Lane near a spring. Just past here, to the right, Bull Ings Lane goes back into the village, or you can continue on Wood Lane.

If you want to go further, follow the river above the Ghaistrills into Grass Wood. The water is quiet and deep in the "Lang Dub," and the house called Netherside Hall, now a school, can be seen among the trees on the other bank. The footpath through the wood comes into Wood Lane, which leads back to the village. Alternatively you can cross the road into the main wood, where there are several paths. Much of the wood is a nature reserve, with a profusion of wild flowers. There are grey squirrels, and many birds. Flowers and plants should not be removed or wildlife disturbed. Visitors should keep to the footpaths and dogs must be kept on a lead.

Edge Top (1½ miles)

This is a walk giving wide views of the dale. At the top of the Main Street, turn right in front of the Town Hall and go up High Lane. This is a narrow, walled, green road, which can be muddy in wet weather. After quarter of a mile, a gate on the left side of the lane leads across the field. There are several stiles, going diagonally across the hillside, and eventually the path joins Edge Lane.

From here you can look across the village to Threshfield Moor and Thorpe Fell. The limestone quarry at Swinden is obvious. Turn left and follow the lane to Spring House, where, down the hill, is Grassington. Opposite Spring House in the old quarry is a seat on a knoll, where you can rest and admire the view.

An extension of this walk can be made. At Spring House go up the hill. The road levels very soon, and on the left is a stile. This crosses a field, then drops down the hillside to join a lane which leads into Chapel Street at the top of the village.

Through Grass Wood (4 miles)

Walk on Chapel Street right to the end, where the signpost at the entrance to Town Head Farm indicates Conistone. Pass through the yard and gate to the right, round the back of the new barn and into the field by a bungalow. Take the lower path down to a stile and into Cove Lane, which terminates in a field. Across the field is Park Stile, a high wooden stile over the wall into the wood. There is a conservation notice here.

Follow the footpath which climbs past an Iron Age settlement and on through the wood, which is largely natural. After half a mile, at the brow of a hill, the public footpath bears right, but it is better to follow the way-marked track down the hill to join the road to Conistone. Turn left at the gate and, in a short while, cross the stile on the right to go back into the wood by the riverside. The path goes past the Ghaistrills and on to Grassington Bridge.

Linton (2½ miles)

Go down to the bridge, cross it, and turn sharp left. Threshfield Old Grammar School is soon reached; at the end of the school playground follow the bridleway to the right. This is the old way to the school from Threshfield. The bridleway joins the road at Monkholme. Cross the road to a stile near some trees, and follow the path down to the beck, crossed by an enormous flagstone.

The path goes under the railway embankment and into a field with Linton Beck to the left. A little gate gives access to a green lane, which passes some old farm buildings and the boundary wall of Linton House to come out by the bridge in Linton. The garden of Linton House, and that of Linton Old Hall, are white with snowdrops in spring. Return by turning left on the road to Great Bank Top crossroads, going straight across and down the hill. Do not turn left at the bottom, but go on to the houses and down the path to the bridge over the river. The Snake Walk leads back to the village.

Skirethorns (3 miles)

This is a pleasant road walk, with no need to worry about wet grass or mud. Threshfield with Skirethorns has a history going back to the times when wolves and bears were common. Caves and barrows have been explored, yielding bones, teeth and skulls of animals, spearheads and earthen vessels. Land was cultivated here before the time of the Normans.

Cross the river bridge and go up the road to Threshfield, passing the Upper Wharfedale Secondary School and the new Roman Catholic Church. Above the school, over the wall, can be seen traces of the old tram track which carried limestone wagons from Threshfield to the railhead at Grassington. Turn right at the little chapel, then very soon cross the road by the petrol station and follow the signpost to Skirethorns. Passing various houses, the road forks at the quarry entrance.

Bear left on the narrow lane, with a couple of attractive stone houses on one side, to the tiny green and a stream. Notice the antlers in the barn entrance just to the right of the road. At the next fork turn left. This pleasant lane passes two farms, and joins another lane which leads to Threshfield Moor. There are wide views across the dale to Grassington.

The lane descends to the main Skipton road and, turning left, Threshfield Bridge is soon reached. Cross this and bear right of the green, past the Manor House with its fine Tudor windows, then right again with Park Grange, an attractive old house, opposite. At the next junction turn left, and in a few minutes you are back in the Grassington road by the tall silo tower.

HEBDEN GILL

Over the Moor to Hebden (5 miles)

This walk takes you on to high ground, with fine views and glimpses of the lead mining relics. From the top of the Main Street, go up Moor Road to the left of the Town Hall. After climbing for 1½ miles, Yarnbury is reached. Turn right, over the cattle grid, and follow the unmade road. There are mine waste heaps alongside, and some old shafts. These are dangerous, and great care should be taken when leaving the path, particularly in misty weather or snow.

When the road forks, keep left, on to a gate with a stile next to it. The road drops to the old dam, damaged in a cloudburst during 1975. On the other side can be seen the smelt mill chimney and the radiating flues. Go back through the stile to the fork, and turn left. The track drops down into Hebden Gill, following the stream, and passing several ruined lead mining buildings. At Hole Bottom the way is through a gate onto a surfaced road which descends into Hebden village. Cross the main road, and passing down the road, with a little school on the left, the fields by the river appear. A signpost by a gate indicates the way. Go through here to the riverside and, turning right, walk upstream to Linton Falls, where the footpath returns to the car park.

Burnsall and Thorpe (6 miles)

From the bottom of the Main Street, turn left on Hebden Road, past the bus station and council estate, until at a sharp bend a narrow lane leads off right. Go down this, passing Low Mill, now converted into a dwelling, and through a gate into a field. There is a good view of Linton Church across the river, and of the rounded hills which are reef knolls. Bear left, across a wooden and sometimes slippery footbridge, and follow the river. In a short while a long row of chestnut trees appears, and then the swing bridge of Hebden.

Cross the bridge and, turning left, the footpath goes down to Burnsall, passing a small limestone gorge called Loup Scar. At the bridge in Burnsall, turn right in front of the Red Lion and go up the road to the bend. Here a footpath is indicated next to a house. This leads into a lane, which should be crossed, and the footpath continues into another lane, which goes to the left and into Thorpe.

Leave by the road in the right corner, and then turn right again. The Burnsall road is soon joined and, following this for a short distance, a stile appears on the right. The footpath crosses the fields diagonally into a green lane by a house, and into the road to Linton Church. Turn left past the car park and mill, then down the footpath to the right which leads to the river and Tin Bridge. Cross this, and the footpath straight ahead takes you back to the village.

This walk can be shortened, omitting Burnsall, by going up the field straight opposite the swing bridge at Hebden. The bridlepath joins the Burnsall road. Straight across is the lane leading into Thorpe.

BURNSALL BRIDGE

Mossdale — a longer fell walk (10 miles)

Boots are necessary unless the ground is very dry.

Go up Moor Road to Yarnbury, and straight up the rough road at the end of the tarmac. In a short distance there is a gate to the left. Through this follow the lane, which soon becomes a footpath, and ignore paths to the right. A lonely farm well away to the left has a track to it. This is Barras, or Bare House, and the views from it are fantastic. However, keep straight on. The height is now nearly 1,400 ft. Eventually a track joins from the left and the way is now under Black Edge into Mossdale, with Great Whernside away to the north. The caverns at Mossdale were the scene of a tragedy a few years ago, six potholers being drowned when the stream rose quickly and flooded the caverns.

Retrace your steps to the junction of the paths, and this time take the right hand one. This descends steeply and joins Bycliffe road down into Coniston. Just past the chapel a footpath goes up the hillside to the left and reaches Dib Scar. Cross this ravine into Lea Green, a huge open area with many limestone outcrops. The footpath skirts the top of Bastow Wood and comes out at Town Head Farm. Pass through the gate, alongside the barn, and turn to the right through another gate into the farmyard which adjoins Chapel Street. Straight on here and you are back at the Town Hall.

Exploring Upper Wharfedale

UPPER WHARFEDALE is one of the most popular of the larger dales of Yorkshire. It is largely limestone country, with fine river scenery, high moors and fells, and several villages providing for the tourist and holidaymaker. The northern part is narrow and wild, with high passes linking with Wensleydale and Coverdale. Littondale, which runs off north-west from just above the spectacular Crag at Kilnsey, has high roads connecting with Malhamdale and Settle. Wharfedale offers a ruined abbey, waterfalls, rapids, ancient churches, unspoilt villages, potholes and some of the finest walking and touring country in England.

Down Dale

Burnsall

B6160. A popular village, with a green and a splendid river bridge, Burnsall has some houses of great antiquity near the church, which dates from the 12th century. Inside the church is a Norse–Danish font, and parts of Anglican crosses. The village stocks are in the churchyard, which is reached through a lychgate, operated by a system of weights. Next to the church is the fine Elizabethan school and master's house. Still in daily use and with little of its frontage altered, the school was founded in 1605 by William Craven of Appletreewick for boys in the parish. As this covered a large area, provision was made for the boys to board. The upper storey was divided into dormitory chambers by oak planks, and this structure is still there.
Inns: The Red Lion, The Fell Hotel.
Cafe. Car park on riverside. Toilets.
Burnsall Sports and Fell Race: Mid-August.

Appletreewick

On minor road on east side of River Wharfe, two miles south of Burnsall. Straggling on each side of the street, the village has several old houses. Monks Hall is on the site of property belonging to Bolton Priory; the pigeon holes and outside stairs are late 17th century. High Hall, at the top of the street, was the home of the Craven family, of which Sir William, born in 1548, is the best known as he became Lord Mayor of London in 1610. The village was once well known for its Onion Fair. There are pleasant riverside walks.
Inns: Craven Arms, New Inn.

Caravan site and camping site near river. Caravan site at Howgill Lodge; also Howarth Farm, Skyreholme, T, MC; Mill Lane, T.

At the road junction beyond Appletreewick, keep straight on to Skyreholme. Upstream is Trollers Gill, a limestone gorge, and across on a hill spur is Percival Hall, a restored Elizabethan house now used as a retreat by the Church of England. It is reputed to have been used by the highwayman William Nevison, from whom many of the Dick Turpin legends have sprung. The gardens are open to the public daily (May to September). Up dale the road from Appletreewick passes through Hartlington.

Barden Tower

B6160. About three miles from Burnsall, the ruined Barden Tower stands to the left. Enlarged from a forest lodge by Henry Lord Clifford of Skipton Castle in the 15th century, the tower was repaired in 1657 by Lady Anne Clifford, but became ruinous after 1774. There is a chapel and an attendant's house. It is possible to see this tower from the outside only. A road leads down to Barden Bridge, a graceful arched 17th century structure. Mason's marks can be seen on the stones. A footpath from here gives entry to the woods and leads downstream to the Strid. There is a small charge.

Bolton Abbey

B6160. The village of Bolton is much older than the famous ruin, which is not an abbey but a priory. Of Anglican origins, the area became the property of a Norman, Robert Romille, who later moved to Skipton and built the castle there.
Car parks in the village. Devonshire Arms Hotel.
Post Office. Cafe.
Caravans: The Strid Wood, T.

Bolton Priory

B6160. Parts of the precinct wall are alongside the road, and 'The Hole in the Wall' gives access to the priory grounds. Alongside the road is Bolton Hall, the shooting lodge of the Duke of Devonshire which was built in the 1850s on the site of the old gatehouse. Near this a narrow arch which restricts speed is an 18th century aqueduct.

The views from the 'hole' over the level, riverside meadow, with the priory ruins, the rectory, the stepping stones and a footbridge, under a high cliff, are splendid. Beyond the river the hills rise to Simon Seat. There are hollows which were the priory's fishponds, and the rectory, built about 1700, includes part of the infirmary. The extensive ruins of the priory include a cloister, frater, chapter house, prior's lodging, and the church, which continued in use after the Dissolution. The present day church is only the nave of the original, but contains much of historic interest. The priory is open daily.

Bolton Woods and the Strid

For two miles or so above the priory, the Wharfe passes through lovely scenery. At the Cavendish Pavilion (refreshments) a toll bridge gives access to the opposite bank, or the path can be followed for a mile to the Strid. This narrow gorge has been the scene of drownings and it is unwise to try to jump across. Road access to Cavendish Pavilion and car park is from the Cavendish Memorial. There is a Nature Trail.

Angling: Tickets from the Estate Offices.

A Journey up the Dale

Kilnsey

B6160. The massive limestone Kilnsey Crag close to the dale road is well known, and the difficult climb over its bulge has been featured on television. The village is small, grouped round an old grange of Fountains Abbey. It was a great sheep centre in monastic days, and the corn from the Abbey lands around was ground here. The flat fields in front of the Crag were the base of a lake, formed after the melting of the glacier which cut the face of the huge rock. There are still important sheep sales held here, and the annual show on the Summer Bank Holiday Tuesday brings big crowds. The race up the Crag attracts entries from a wide area. The steep green road running from the head of the village is Mastiles Lane, which goes over the tops to Malham Tarn.

Inn: The Tennants Arms.
Angling: Tickets from Tennants Arms. Trout Farm.

Conistone

Across the river bridge, which is very old, is Conistone, a cluster of houses and a church. Behind the village is a narrow limestone gorge, and a lane climbs up to the flanks of Great Whernside at Mossdale. Some of the houses are 17th century. The church is of Saxon foundation and has two massive round arches on the north side of the nave. The roads lead to Grassington and Kettlewell.

Post Office.

Half a mile above Kilnsey there is a road junction — the left road is to Littondale, and the main dale road is to Kettlewell. Across the valley can be seen a group of buildings with a Scandinavian style church; this is Scargill House, a Church of England centre.

Kettlewell

B6160, 6m from Grassington. Of ancient origins and having thriving times in monastic days, Kettlewell belonged to the Nevilles of Middleham in 1605.

It became Crown property until Charles I granted it to some London merchants who sold it to local people. The Manor is still governed by the Trust Lords who are elected from the Freeholders. Although many of the older houses have been altered, the bridge is splendid, and the beck from Cam Gill and Dowber Gill runs between the houses. The church was rebuilt in the 19th century.

The steep and twisty road from the head to the village climbs Park Rash and goes over to Coverdale and Middleham. In Park Gill, at the foot of Park Rash is Dow Cave, which can be explored for a short distance if care is taken. There are several fine walks in the area.

Inns: The Bluebell, The Racehorses, The King's Head.
Post Office and shop. Garage. Youth Hostel.
Early closing: Thursday.
Angling: tickets from Tennants Arms Hotel, Kilnsey.
Caravans: Causeway Croft, T.

Starbotton

2m from Kettlewell, B6160. The road up the dale is close to the river here. The hillsides are patterned with limestone walls, running from the level meadows on the valley floor to the tops of the fells. Isolated outbarns are dotted here and there. The village of Starbotton is all grey limestone, weathered and coloured with moss. The houses are mainly 17th century, although several have been modernised and are used as holiday homes. In 1686 a great flood swept away many of the dwellings. The green road behind the village climbs up the Knuckle Bone to the summit of Buckden Pike.

Inn: Fox and Hounds.

Buckden

B6160, 10m from Grassington. A small village in an important position at the junction of two roads, Buckden derives its name from the deer that once lived in the area and was the residence of the officers of Langstrothdale forest. Buckden Pike (2,302 feet) is above the village. There are some old cottages, a car park and picnic area. The B6160 goes to Cray, and then over Kidstones Pass to Bishopdale and Aysgarth. The other road, to the left from the small green, leads into Langstrothdale and over Fleet Moss to Hawes in Wensleydale.

Inn: The Buck.
Post Office and shop.
Angling: Tickets from The Buck Inn.

Hubberholme

At Kirk Gill, 1m from Buckden, is the fine Hubberholme church, and across the bridge, the George Inn, once the vicarage. The massive church tower is 13th century, and inside there is a rare rood screen dating from 1558. The pews are by a modern craftsman, Thompson of Kilburn, known as the

Upper Wharfedale panorama. This sweeping view looks down-dale towards Grass Wood, with the River Skirfare on the left and Kilnsey Crag on the right.

'Mouseman.' On the church side of the river, a road joins that from Buckden in Cray Gill. At **Cray,** a tiny hamlet with some nearby waterfalls, is the White Lion Inn, where the antlers of the last deer to be killed in the valley are to be seen.

Yockenthwaite

Updale from Hubberholme the river flows through open land — a popular place for picnics. Before dropping to Yockenthwaite bridge the road passes the farm of Raisgill, behind which is the old green road, the Horse Head Pass, to Foxup in Littondale. Yockenthwaite, of Norse origins, is now a tiny hamlet, but there are records of other houses, an inn and a school. On the north side of the river, just beyond the houses, is a Bronze Age stone circle with twenty stones standing on edge. The river here has cut rock pools and little gorges in the limestone. There are few trees, and the dale is wild and beautiful. A little bridge crosses the river at Deepdale, where there is a group of old farmhouses. There is an Iron Age village on the west side of Deepdale Gill, about 1,600 feet up.

Oughtershaw

A mile or so further up the dale, Oughtershaw Beck joins the one from Greenfield to form the river Wharfe, and at the junction is the hamlet of Beckermonds. The road to the right from the junction of the becks leads into Oughtershaw, which stands at 1,200 feet. The hall, in a deep gorge, is fairly modern, and the small school was built in 1847 by the Woodd family, who lived in the hall. The road continues over Fleet Moss to Hawes, but the old track by the beck goes to Cam Houses, where it joins the Roman road from Bainbridge. The Fleet Moss road gives spectacular views, but it is steep in places and quickly affected by snow or mist.

Littondale

The flat bottomed glacial valley, which was once called Amerdale, runs off to the north-west about half a mile above Kilnsey. The river in the dale is the Skirfare, which joins the Wharfe at Hammerdale Dub. The limestone fells climb steeply from the valley, and geology students will find plenty of interest. There is a road on either side — the one on the left runs straight to Arncliffe, the other passing through Hawkswick.

Hawkswick

The village has some old buildings near the river. A bridge leads across the dale to Hawkswick and Arncliffe Cotes, which were former granges of Fountains Abbey and are still sheep farms. There is a caravan site here.

Arncliffe

This is the principal village in the dale. It clusters round a green, and has a fine old church next to the river. An old corn mill at the far end of the green has been converted into flats. Cowside Beck runs alongside it from Malham Moor, passing through a wild gorge, Yew Cogar Scar. The inn, the Falcon, was for many years the home of Marmaduke Miller a well known Dales artist. The house at Bridge End, with a lawn running down to the river, was favourite place of Charles Kingsley during the time he stayed at Malham Tarn and conceived *The Water Babies*. The church has been largely restored but the tower is Norman. Inside is a list of the Arncliffe men who fought at the Battle of Flodden in 1513. A steep, twisty road from the village leads to Malham (10m), Langcliffe, and then to Settle. It passes the remote Darnbrook Farm in a steep little valley.

Inn: The Falcon.
Amerdale House Hotel. Cafe. Post Office.

Litton

This small village gives its name to the dale. It is two miles from Arncliffe, and has some 17th century houses. A track climbs over to Hubberholme, and from the bridge, a short distance up river, a green road mounts the fell and joins the motor road from Halton Gill.

Inn: The Queen's Arms.
Post Office.

Halton Gill

Overshadowed by great fells, this hamlet consists largely of 17th century houses. The road across the river climbs between Fountains Fell and Penyghent, over wild sheep country, into Stainforth, with the Ribblesdale road then going into Settle. Above Halton Gill is **Foxup,** where the road ends.

Motor Runs from Grassington

THE village is a good centre for touring the Yorkshire Dales National Park. Many places of interest in Yorkshire are within a couple of hours' driving. In the Dales be prepared for hills, some of them steep and winding. In bad weather the higher roads may be enveloped in cloud and winds can be very strong. Petrol stations are fairly numerous, although some close on Sundays and few are open after 6 p.m. The Dalesman's Yorkshire Dales Map (½ inch) is useful.

Upper Nidderdale: 35 miles

Drive on Hebden Road, B6265, which turns left when coming down the Main Street. This passes through Hebden and climbs to Greenhow, one of the county's highest villages, with many lead mining relics. On the way you drop down to Dibbles (Devils) Bridge, the scene of a terrible coach disaster in 1975, and climb up Fancarl, passing Stump Cross Caverns which are open daily in summer. From Greenhow the road descends into Nidderdale, with fine views, and approaches Pateley Bridge. Just opposite the garage turn left; very soon a large water wheel can be seen and then the Wath road end. Just past this, Gouthwaite appears on the right. This natural looking lake is a reservoir and a haunt of wild fowl.

At the head of the lake is Ramsgill, followed by Lofthouse. A short way after this village, which had a station on the light railway used in the 1920s when the reservoirs were built, a road leads off left to How Stean Gorge. There are several rapids and waterfalls to be seen. There is a car park and refreshments.

Higher up still, the road ends at Middlesmoor with fine views of the dale from the churchyard at over 900 ft. Returning on the same road, turn off left at Wath and continue on the hillside to Pateley Bridge, a quaint town with a narrow main street and a ruined church high on the hillside. From here the way back is via Greenhow.

Malham: 30 miles

Malham is an ancient village set in magnificent limestone scenery, and is reached by a drive over the high uplands. From Grassington go to Threshfield, turn right up the Kettlewell road past Kilnsey Crag, and bear left at the fork for Arncliffe. At the far end of the green the road crosses the beck and climbs very steeply on to the moor, passing the deep ravine of Yew Coggar Scar on the left. A very steep descent follows, with hairpin bends, to the bridge at Darnbrook House. After another climb the road reaches a height of 1,341 ft. — there are gates to open — and soon Malham Tarn can be seen on the left. Turn left at the next fork, and then after passing High Trenhouse Farm left again. The Tarn can be reached by a short walk over the moor.

The road continues past the Tarn and descends into Malham village. There is a large car park, with toilets, at the far end of the village, and the National Park Centre. This is well worth a visit. Malham Cove and Gordale Scar, unique in limestone scenery, are within walking distance.

Return by driving down Malhamdale through Kirkby Malham, with an interesting old church, Airton and Eshton, with a sharp left turn a short distance after the gates of Eshton Hall. The road then goes through Flasby into Hetton, and on to Cracoe and the Grassington road.

Wensleydale: 55 miles

Go up the dale to Kettlewell, Starbotton and Buckden. Bear right here to climb over Kidstones Pass and then through Bishopdale to Aysgarth, where the waterfalls on the river Ure are famous.

From Aysgarth drive on the A684 through West Witton and Wensley to Leyburn, a market town. From here follow the A6108 across the river to Middleham, a racehorse centre with a massive ruined castle (the boyhood home of Richard III). The route from Middleham climbs through Coverdale in wild country by the flanks of Great Whernside (2,310 ft.) and descends very steeply, with sharp bends, into Kettlewell. At the bottom of the village turn left and follow the road into Conistone, passing Grass Wood to return to Grassington.

A diversion from Aysgarth to Bolton Castle, well worth a visit, can be made via Carperby, Redmire, and into Leyburn.